LANES OF LIFE

A BUNCH OF POEMS FROM VARIOUS LANES OF LIFE.

NANDANA KRISHNA

To my family, my dear friends and all wellwishers this little development wouldn't be possible without the love and support of yours. Thank god, for all the opportunities and blessings. Last but not the least, dear readers thankyou for choosing to flip pages through the poems of this book.

Contents

Foreword

I am still a student figuring out what professional career I will have to pursue.

It was on a late afternoon, in a boring lecture I found a piece of paper lying near my foot. Out of curiosity

when I picked up the paper, there were some quotes written on it. Out of them there was one in particular

that caught my attention, it read like this "I know the value of love, because I know the oain of hatred".

I believe it was written by a friend of mine, I don't know if it was imitated from somewhere else. This quote

that struck to my mind and triggered the poet in me. Almost a year later, I wrote my very first poem

and showed my friends. The support of theirs was great, it inspired me to write more, and so started this

journey of being in love with writing, watchin and hearing things through soul and not just by eyes and

ears.

Five years later today when am all serious about poetry, and full of hopes all I ask to the readers is for

your support, love and prayers. I hope this very first work of mine wins your love!

Preface

This book contains a collection of a few poems I have written through the course of past 3 years. Each poem would take you through the phases of life a commoner can relate to, usually to their late teen age. As said, the teen age of anyone's life is a furnace of emotions. Often teenage is tallied to the first love, the confusion, the bitter lessons, colourful friendships and campus lives, and many more to list on.

The poems are basically fictional, yet I have taken references to real life happenings I had walked through. I have worked my best to present the sketch of situations in words just like a summary, to make the poetry sound more meaningful. I hope the efforts taken had fruited sweet, giving you a great read time.

Thank you!

Acknowledgements

"Gratitude", a word that has so much emotions and an emotion itself. Today

when my dream of past few years near the light of reality, I can't move forward without

thanking the people who walked with me as a companion, as a support and as encouragement till date.

Let me thank my mother, for being supportive and constantly backing me for publishing my first

book. Thanking my father, who taught me through his life, the art of viewing from the soul

which is a very crucial skill needed for an artist. Can't move foreward without thanking my little brother

for his innocent appreciations for anything I do, also for being a content for my poetry at times.

Let me take a moment to thank my teachers, who had sowed in me the seeds of all goodness,

knowledge and passion. Without them, I am sure, I would have never reached anywhere atleast

till wherever I am now.

I also would like to take this space for thanking my dear friends, without them walking this far would

have never been possible. From spending time to read my works, to reminding me always to go forward with this dream. They had always been there, to lift me up and inspire me to keep working. It'd be unfair

to miss anyone in the list of friends, so I am not risking to name them here. I owe you so much gratitude

and pray that we shall all be parts of eachother's life forever.

Let me thank, notion press for this opportunity. For a student like me, who is keen in publishing writeups

it's not just enough for having a right publishing group, but also to have it in an affordable pricing.

Thank you team, for it's only because of you the poems in my paper would be reaching to the soul of

readers.

Last but not the least, thank god for whatever life has been till now, praying for everyone's goodness and

joy.

Thankyou!

1. Vines of pubescence

"Plot: Pubescence or the teen age is a period of life that turns out to be the most important for any person. Scientifically speaking major developments and changes take place during this phase of life. Well , some of us also relate to the various psychological changes when we speak about teen age. This is all about that."

The smooth growth was accelerated abruptly.
There were waves inside searching for new shores.
The tides of teen age were not low,
just like the kid's energy it was all in the peak no matter anger or joy.
Till then the kids, now feel like grown though actually they aren't.
They were flowers with tender petals
fluttering in the storms of emotions. Their hearts pounded,
as if it found a new sensed energy.
Just like the vines of climbers they climbed, in the race for their aim.
The tenderness was occasionally tested,
to make them bear the harsher storms of life. On the way,

they climb the poles of love, poor they not knowing love is an ocean

not a pole.

Red as blood, true as fire love they mistook to be their only purpose of life.

Not knowing love is a cyclone, not the storm that's raging now they shed away

all that they own. They cause scars on the tenderness and wail over it,

unaware that the scars are the like the bitter manures for climbing high.

As they pass over this phase of teen time, they flourish in the colours of success.

Though it gifted some pain, they'd remember the days later with a smile.

2. Prisoner she

"Plot: She is a girl, just around any of us. When she makes the world around her loved ones bearable, she falls into the invisible prison of love. Even when the bundle of commitments get heavy for her to fly high, she holds on to the love for her dear ones."

She is just another unheard story, a concealed story of wounds beneath the deepest layers of soul.

She is a prisoner, behind the bars of everyone's love. That's how she still breathes,

in the strength of her love for all. She is a prisoner,

for her choices are weighed in the scale of society's measure of right and wrong.

Out of love she had, she altered her choice to what the society defined would be right.

She is a prisoner in the dreams she reconstructed according to the plans of those she loved.

All she wanted was their smile, and them to be pleased at the instant.

She is a prisoner even now, in the gestures to words that could please someone she loved.

For once she wishes, if she could fly in the sky of her limit, in the stroke of flight she chose.

She was a prisoner, yes with all amenities but freedom. She was smart,

but not daring enough to speak about her smartness. Love is what made her a coward.

Even when she wipes the tears and worries of her dear ones, she keeps her tears to the room of her heart.

She just wishes to peep into the world's treasure of wonders by travelling.

She just wanted to be another bird, out of the cage, out of the set limits.

Just to be away into the world's stage , free from those evitable boundaries.

If you ever find her among your crowd, trust me your love can set her free,

and you'll rejuvenate with her love . Not just because she loves, but for

she smiled at everything that broke her and caged her with a heart full of unending love.

3. Starlight, a disguised belssing.

"Plot: For a girl, her dad is a man she can run to at any phase of life. She may grow into a young woman, but for her dad she can always run back as that little kid. Not all of us are lucky, to walk with our dad atleast till we become parents. This is a poem of a girl who loses her dad unexpectedly, and then personifies the star in the sky as her dad in disguise."

Can sky return a star, the fate stole?
She promises the sky, it wouldn't loose the lusture even if it returns this one star for her.
Though this is so kiddish for the dad's bold woman,
but she misses the arms she could always fall asleep in,
she misses the laugh that made life more sonorus.
The warmth of that caressing strokes on head, is what she craves at every lows now.

When his breath was stolen to light up the sky tonight, her freedom was arrested to face life.

When his absence made a home dumb, his void filled in voices of chaos and despair.

Atleast in the heart of one man, she knew she was there without him reassuring.

As she covers many more miles in this journey of life, breathe gets heavier thoughts get cluttered .

The more heavier she breathes, when she realises there's no shoulder to lean on.

She has to keep running, she can't cling to the uncertainities and thir worries.

As dad shines up in the sky, she has to light up this world with the essence of love he shared.

With the strength of a vanished smile, and the starlight as her blessing she sails forward

to the port , life has set as her destiny.

4. From this dusk to poetry.

"Plot: An attempt to elucidate the evening."

The leaves seem pasted to the blue sky. The wind brings fragrance of the wild,
it makes one so high. As the sun conceals and makes way,
for the stars, for the moon to make magic, to wake night.
The cuckoos and crows, the blades of leaf, all the sounds of nature's music,
adorned by a tint of yellow, blanket of pink. The sky looks picture perfect.
Birds are in a hurry, to meet their mates , to settle in their nests.

Just like a glass of drink, this bit of poetry is. Through the veins of this linguaphile,

itseems to be there in every breathe, in every blink and is high in each vein.

Just like the sky paints vivid hues , mind inks thoughts as poetry.

Every poet writes about the rawest emotions, the way their hearts elate,

the shine they have on their love and the way the little things dwell in them.

To be the apple of their eyes, is to experience love in it's purest forms, to live for an eternity.

5. The horrendous hooligan

"Plot: There was a period when the world froze, it took a pause amidst the terrifying attack of a virus, the COVID-19. This poem is about that period."

Rage of earth is cruel now. Vengeance is of a new form, a hoorendous life form.

It multiplied into a swarm, from one corner of the globe to all directions.

If you crowd around, beware it shall mock you down into the infectious trap.

Many who ignored, welcomed a tresspasser who sowed death.

The earth has witnessed brooks of blood, she has heard chinks of swords.

She still bears the remnants of war stories of past. All around the world,

everyone had been keen conquering and protesting. Nature's water and fire,

had places swallowed by them. Now this new enemy, called the pandemic swallowed world

in a whole. A pause was the need, no knowing till when.

Being as small as the farthest star, he pushed the world into anxiety faster than the hurricane.

He helped death gulp away a too many lives at once. Every land that held pride of divinity,

might of power and grandeur of money became graveyards of it's countrymen.

Angels in white battling fate to save lives, guardians of law clearing crowds .

The world is like never before in this pause of worry, of fear, of survival.

6. Each day withered.

"Plot: Days of breakup in her terms. The pain of an unrequitted love is what this poem takes you through."

In the boat of lonliness she was left, with his memories paddling journey forward.

A spring that blossome love ended with her wither into an unseen void.

A destructive storm washed away the love she had, leaving her broken.

It's been long since her cheeks dried. Since too long she wears a smile of strength.

Now as each day withers, she choses to leave her questions unanswered.

As the time passed, it wiped away the pain of separation.

Though the day had parts without his thoughts, at times he'd pop up.

All she was left with was memories, of them that paints colours of separation now.

The eyes that gave piercing gaze, never turned to her now. In the joy of a new love, his eyes widened in glee. In the hope of getting over, she continued to live.

7. Just to live a day of my dreams.

"Plot: Often, a girl is expected to maintain home, be an introvert and society's checklist

goes on. Every girl has a wish to live the life of her dreams, and here's a poem

of a girl's dream life."

The life in dreams is an entirely different one.

Worries for something else, love for something else, hate for something else.

Of the deepest desires, wishing to find the best hues,

just to paint a rainbow of my dreams.

Want to glee at the moon as if it's for the first time.

Want to feel the night breeze, hugging myself tight.

Want to hear the night's tales as the owls talk.

Nothing more, in the era of haste, I just want a day of stagnance,

a breath of calmness, a smile of satisfaction and a boquet of sweet memories.

In the day light, roaming around the busy streets,

peeping into the tiny shops. I just want to roam like a nomad,

for one day without the pressure of goals. Want to run into
the common man,
his little joys, mourns and rage through the busy streets,
collecting the spices of a commoner's life.
While this day in dreams is a distant star,
I'm still insecure for the vultures in search of woman's flesh.
Whatever maybe, I still wish to live this day, the day in my
dreams.

8. To hate you.

"Plot: There are people in our life whom we don hate,
even after doing us wrong.
We forgive and don't carry grudge, for the love we had.
What if the wrongings don't
end with us? What if this person wrongs someone else?
Into the poetry of such a situation."

To hate you and your memories,
to ignore the warmth of your presence, I still have many reasons.
In the woods of reality I am wandering in search of you.
Puzzled I am if I understood you well, or you wore a mask to win
trust.
To hate you and your memories, there are blames, to prove you
accused,
there are facts. But look at me, wandering in the gorge of lost love
searching for what I beleived you to be. When the world accused
you,
I was with you. Now when you turn out to repeat the same deed,
what should I justify you as? I can tolerate you for my tears,
but can't stand another girl's tears of your betrayal.
Tied to the strings of commitments, gratitude and promise,

I couldn't choose you and instead let you go. Frowning at you with all the hate,
I discovered how much we were meant to be. Besides the curses that fall on you now,
I am blanketing you with my prayers,
for you shall rectify the err of betrayal.

9. To the moon, smiling at her.

Now she lacks purpose, she feels vexed up.
A girl with headstrong ambitions, found reasons.
She found excuses to contempt her.
She was in a war with the fumes inside her.
Smiling bright, proving happy she is, she smiles to hide.
She once wants to break down, on a safe shoulder.
She wants to raise herself up to her expectations.
A girl with priceless values, wants to build an identitiy that defines her.
Though the woman in her wants to roar in success, the girl in her is meek.
She wants to pour out the love for the one,
The guilt of mistakes so far eats her up to darkness.
The insecurities inside knock her down, while she tries to stand stiff.
Knowing she is not the same strong girl,
she speaks to the moon hoping it's listening to her.
After every talk, she believes the moon has sent strength for the girl in her,

to grow into the woman of her expectations. The moon seems smiling,
to confront her fears, itseems to be tha armour in fornt of her insecurities.

10. And, we diverged

"Plot: Days of breakup is a tougher battle. She tells him all she goes through"

We never knew how we met. Nor did we know when our eyes forgot to talk.

As each moment flew away like feathers so light , the distance our soul went,

apart seemed so heavy. We were beside each other, when my tears for you burned my cheeks.

For me, our memories is a coffin ,

it pulls me back to the strangest truth of love gifting the pain of dying ad infinitum.

Well my world still showers love, without you in it. To give them back where shall I go,

for my ocean of love is all dried by pouring itself into you. In the densest thickets of life,

all I have is myself, after losing you, losing an old good me, losing my love and what else is left.

All am left with is this breath that gets hefty with every moment in your absence.

With this left, am wandering in search of words, in the hunt of rythms for , it shall describe the love I have, and I had.

11. Here and there.

"Plot: A person discovering that they are prone to daydream. Understands that
they are affected with maladaptive daydreaming narrates a poem about themself, their life."

I can feel the pearls of my crown becoming loose.
I can feel the lusture of my life bcoming dull.
I can see the future hardly breathing, it's being lead to a prison of
pause.
Caught in the cage of vivid thoughts,
I live a beautiful life in my daydreams. The fantasy gives so much
releif.
People are kind and real there,
the warmth of love is always found. Waking into reality,
am all alone. Slowly I cease to exist in the real world,
walking into my fantasies forgetting about my duties here.
In the paths of danger, he accompanies me,
he holds my hands and hugs me tight, don't know where he is in
reality.
The warmth in fantasies have never reached me,
there am always appreciated and understood by everyone around.
Here I struggle to understand me, my needs and thoughts.

Though I live here, I love being there.
Leaving the lines unconcluded, am rushin there to breathe some
relaxation.

12. The last breathe, without air.

"Plot: Back during the COVID times, there was a short period when we faced
oxygen shortage at our hospitals. Into the poetry of this horrifying situation that once
shook our country."

The world is becoming quiet again, children at home wondering about their stagnant childhood.

Well, a pause to childhood is ok . But what if there's no air at the verge of death.

At a place where death and life meets, where would a common man go to find the life's support.

No, this isn't blame. These are the summaries of heartbreaking stories.

Once a father who walked into the toys store, is now cluelessly running for the life gas.

Who knows if he could keep the pulse of his daughter after all the run.

The son who longed to gift his first earning to his mother, is busy borrowing , to meet expenses for providing every human's right of breath to his mother.

While burrial grounds become dump yards, there are those people who walk carelessly.

There are people who wound the angels serving humanity, with no mercy and scarce gratitude.

The virus isn't a monster to be your nightmare, but it surely is a cause of ache.

Prevent and pray, there are people who turn out to be orphans in this period,

in the lack of the life gas, in the reign of this tiny little being.

13. Beauty

"Plot: Attempting to describe beauty."

In the smallest efforts that gifts real happiness, I find you.

In the cuddles of love and deep eye talks I find you.

In the clothes that gifts me his fragrance, I find you.

Deep down, I yearn for him knowing he is my happy fantasy.

I know our love is something yet to happen, he is someone I haven't found yet.

Keeping all the love for him unshared to anyone else, I feel you in me.

You define the real, you define us. You are what I call beauty, unseen though, I can feel you in every moment of being me.

14. The love still resides.

"Plot: Describing rain, in the perspective of a poet.
Through the lanes life took each one of us."

The air here fills the soul with the breeze that smells rain.

The rain that sweeps mud, sweeps her thoughts to the past.

Gazing at the might of rain, wandering in the past's pain.

*She walked through the muddy life, struggling to keep each step
forward.*

Now she smells the nature, it's freshness.

The quietitude is spellbound, with the echoing sound of rain.

The birds and leaves, just like her are in awe of rain's might.

*She could now smile at the tears of past, though the rain was in
rage.*

*As the might slowly weakened , she recalled the old folk of rain
being sky's kiss to the ground.*

Soon the sound of rain halted, and birds took over to chirp.

*There was the sound of a distant laughter and some good old
tunes.*

*The rain would return with sky's kiss, maybe mightier than before
or meaker.*

*Her love for rain would multiply each time it returns, and this
continues thereafter.*

15. First Love

"Plot: This short poem is about a girl whose first love ceased by the death of her dear one. To this world she is a girl who smiles always, but in her heart she has stories of pain unsaid. "

He was the star she looked through the window before heading to sleep.

He is the one who left to gaze the world of his from far away , in the dark sky.

Without bidding the last bye, without the last smile he left her in the chaos of a childhood love.

He fell into her life, when she never knew what love was. They were denied to be tied to the strings of love,

but still held to each other just like in a fantasy.

There was a sudden pause, they never had a sight or heard eachother for quite long.

Though there was love that they had for eachother in them, they couldn't connect, couldn't communicate.

One day that rose up like the red sun of misfortune, all she heard was that he left to a world far away.

Some roses were the last fragrance she could gift him, still through the open window into the eternal soul of her first love.

16. Walk into my completeness, if you can.

"Plot: When you find the hopes of a new love, but the scars of your first love is just dried. Though you want to know if the love would work out, you choose to keep quiet because of the bitter past, to save a friendship and in chaos if it'd ruin the existing good bonds."

I don't wanna bear more scars, or cause them in you.
I don't fear rejection, but I do fear a possible separation.
Staying dumb to the wails of my heart is cowardice, I know. But I can't dare to lose you.
There might come a day when you walk on to be someone's , and now I've to forsee that.
Though I am not sure if the drum beat in me is the tune of love, I fear my heart.
What if it pleads for you at a time when we can't come together?
Now don't ask me what love is, if this isn't. Am in the cat's cradle of emotions, caught up in your thoughts.
So now, I choose to walk into a dungeon, with the twilight of your thoughts.
As I move deeper, I believe there will be some flickering to the twilight,

*and once the twilight is blown off, I would find light and that
being the end of this labyrinth.*

*I never want you to walk into my life's void, if we ever walk
together walk into my completeness.*

*I am broken, I know into pieces that would glue up in the care
and attention you give*

*but no, I don't want you to fix them up either. The shattered me
is healing on it's own,*

*walk into as the scars dry, they would glow up if there is a shower
of your love.*

-Nandana Krishna

17. That Night

"*Plot: It's for the first time she witnesses a native festive night. In India, most temples host annual festivities. The fireworks, rituals and people's vigour is a must to witness. What if a festive night is elucidated as a poem, in the view of a student who witnesses it for the very first time? Well, this poem is about a festive night.*"

The lights from earth reached sky with a thud.
The dark sky had more than stars and moon to make it adorable with some bright colours.
The strings of violins and beats of drums was so much in rythm, a big crowd was seen dancing that day.
That night we stood on the roadsides admiring the sky with the sonorus temple bands,
these roads never seemed interesting when we usually walk to classes.
An elephant walked with grandeur, the crowd was a pack of trmemndous energy.
Till then the bookworms, suddenly outshone the folk dancers to the beats of musicians.

An evening stepped into night, as the elephant walked to the temple pool.

Those moments when the music band skipped into fast numbers, got forever sealed in our hearts.

It was for the first time, the eyes witnessed a festive night.

Those moments are now a new hue to the ribbon of colourful memories.

To add beauty to the memories, some friends got tightly sealed into wonderful bonds.

18. I wish, you were here.

"Plot: This girl with so much love, wishes if her one was there with her on a rainy day.
This poem is all about how she yearns for him."

On this rainy day, I wish you were here.
We and this path that put us together drenched in rain.
Ground is wet and the air smells rain.
It's all rain here, around me. Inside me, it's raining love.
On this eve that pours rain, I wish we were together, here.
Me, you and the tall umbrella, along the half worn path.
The slush on the roads dirtying our boots, and with each step forward splashing the water on ground.
As the winds pull away the wet hair strands and we stealing a quick gaze,
the gaze slipping away into a timid smile. Quitting my fears of thunder in the courage of your love,
I wish you were her, with me on this rainy day.

19. Love and ambition.

"*Plot: A woman is both a lover and the proffessional.*
Her life has to be a space for both
love and career. Into the poetic interpretation of how
life of a woman focuses or needs to
focus on both."

Can she not fall in love again to be protected from further wounds?

Can she still hope to find the cure for her wounded soul?

Through the scripts she writes, she keeps floating in this wave of life.

Faster than feathers, everyone entering life withers.

Though this has become usual, she still gives her all.

Once again when all hopes dry, she falls tiredly asleep in the lap of self love.

In a world that is as vivid as the wings of a butterfly, she is vivid herself,

being kind and humane. Through her poems she whispers her love for him,

loud enough for this world to hear. Though she hasn't met the one, she is in love.

Not just at the thoughts of him, but in the determination too her eyes glisten.

Not just the notes of love, but there are plans for a successful career too in her.

Not just to discover layers of love, but also to hunt down the challenges of competition she is keen.

She may seem a random romanticist, yes she is one such real romantic.

She is also a woman warring each day to conquer heights of career.

20. Somewhere, in the path.

Somewhere in the old path I am stuck, still. It soesn't mean I stand still,

it's that my heart still wanders around there. The path we had walked down together,

it's far away from here. It is a path I'd never perhaps walk back again,

but still I visit that narrow road with green blankets.

As loud as that festive night, today I scream to my mind to come back, to stay here.

I don't wander there in search of an unrequited love, I know it isn't about the kind of fantasy love.

Some point in the path pulls me back to the days we were near, I wish to be blindfolded

*from there till here, atleast to forget this unusual attachment to
you and the old path
and every string that ties.
Still sometimes warring between wanting to stay attached and
searching what we are,
I flutter in the memories we painted in the direction of a chaotic
blow of thoughts.
I wonder why am sure not in love, but so attached to the thought
of you.*

Towards More Love And Light!

This had been a dream since my pen inked poetry. To publish a book of my poems.

I shall once again take this space to thank every one who had walked with me in the lanes of my life,

holding me tight, encouraging me, inspiring me and passing the love and light in you to me.

My parents, who had taught me the values of love, of being kind, of being observant. They who

had beleived in my every step, and still support to acheive more, they are the ones who had been

prominent in inspiring me at every step till date.

Let me thank my friends who took time to read every poem of mine, irrespective of the time when I

streched out it to them. They who always assured me of the quality in my works if at all I feel low.

Let me thank the people who were the reasons for my first unexpected published work, in an anthology.

I owe you my deepest and most sincere gratitude.

Last but not the least, to the people whom my book is sent, to the lovely audience

It's after so much hope and wait, this book is reaching you. I have made this as wonderful it can be by

rendering every possible effort from my side. I hope as you flip through the pages, you understand the soul of a poet's perspective. I also kindly ask you to pardon me for any mistakes that I've failed to notice.

Towards more love and light,

Nandana Krishna.